RIVER FOREST PUBLIC LIBRARY
735 Lathrop Avenue
River Forest, Illinois 60305
708 / 366-5205

Smithsonian

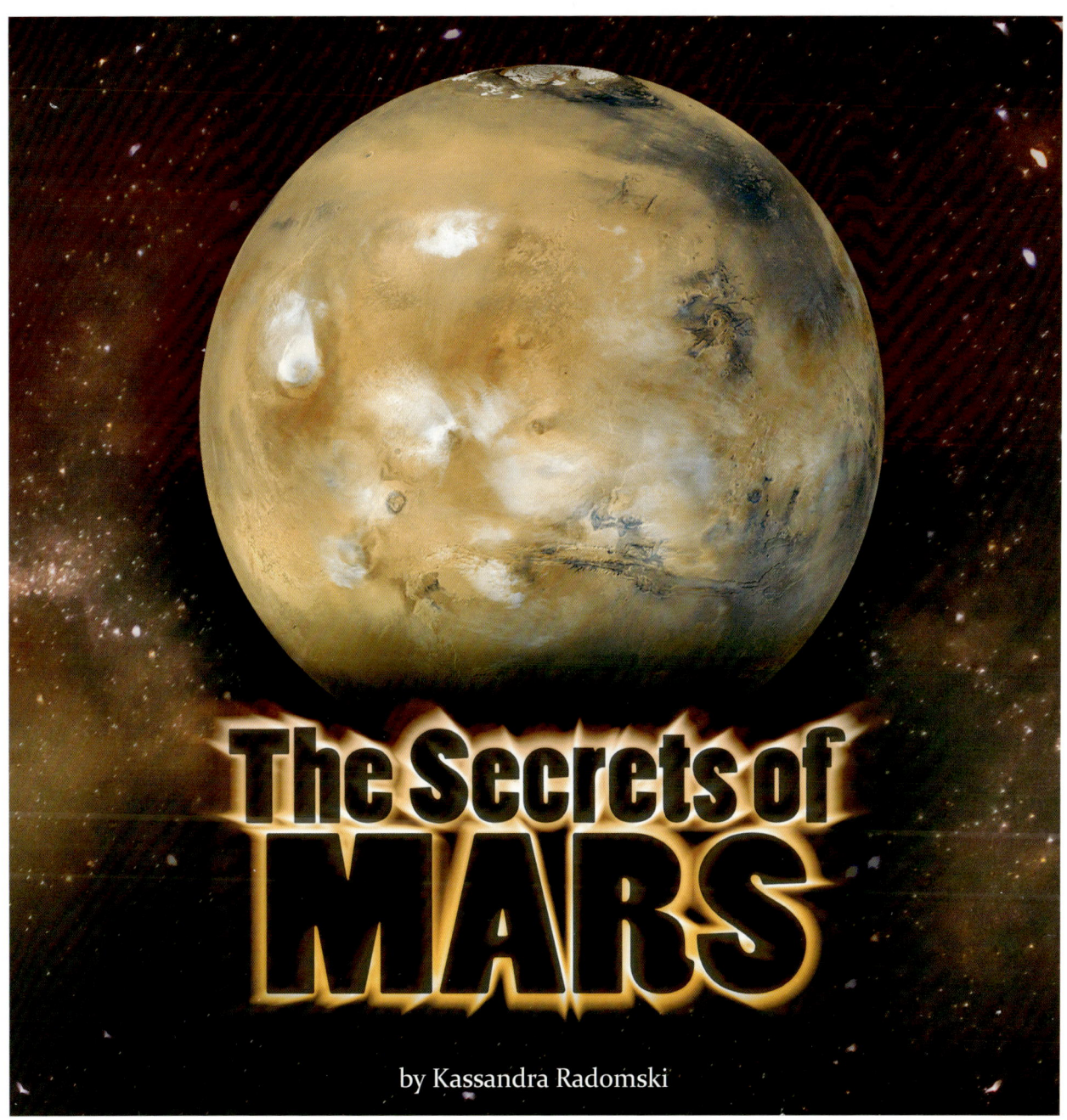

The Secrets of MARS

by Kassandra Radomski

CAPSTONE PRESS
a capstone imprint

Capstone Press
1710 Roe Crest Drive, North Mankato, Minnesota 56003
www.capstonepub.com

Copyright © 2016 by Capstone Press, a Capstone imprint. All rights reserved. No part of this publication may be reproduced in whole or in part, or stored in a retrieval system, or transmitted in any form or by any means, electronic, mechanical, photocopying, recording, or otherwise, without written permission of the publisher.

The name of the Smithsonian Institution and the sunburst logo are registered trademarks of the Smithsonian Institution. For more information, please visit www.si.edu.

Library of Congress Cataloging-in-Publication Data
Radomski, Kassandra, author.
 The secrets of Mars / by Kassandra Radomski.
    pages cm. — (Smithsonian. Planets)
 Summary: "Discusses the planet Mars, including observations by ancient cultures, current knowledge of Mars, and plans for future scientific research and space exploration"—Provided by publisher.
  Audience: Ages 8-10.
  Audience: Grades 2 to 4.
  Includes index.
  ISBN 978-1-4914-5865-5 (library binding)
  ISBN 978-1-4914-5898-3 (paperback)
  ISBN 978-1-4914-5909-6 (eBook PDF)
 1. Mars (Planet)—Juvenile literature. 2. Mars (Planet)—Exploration—Juvenile literature. I. Title.
  QB641.R33 2016
  523.43—dc23   2014044208

Editorial Credits
Elizabeth R. Johnson, editor; Tracy Davies McCabe and Kazuko Collins, designers;
Wanda Winch, media researcher; Tori Abraham, production specialist

Our very special thanks to Andrew K. Johnston, Geographer, Center for Earth and Planetary Studies, National Air and Space Museum, Smithsonian Institution, for his curatorial review. Capstone would also like to thank Kealy Gordon, Smithsonian Institution Product Development Manager, and the following at Smithsonian Enterprises: Ellen Nanney, Licensing Manager; Brigid Ferraro, Director of Licensing; Carol LeBlanc, Senior Vice President, Consumer & Education Products; Chris Liedel, President.

Photo Credits
Black Cat Studios: Ron Miller, 9, 11, 12, 15; Lunar and Planetary Institute, 5 (bottom); NASA: 17, 29, J. Bell (Cornell U.) and M. Wolff (SSI), 10, JPL, 17 (top), 10, 20, JPL/MSSS, cover, back cover, 1, 5 (top), JPL-Caltech, 25, 27, JPL-Caltech/ASU/UA, 14, JPL-Caltech/Cornell Univ./Arizona State Univ., 21, JPL-Caltech/MSSS, 24, JPL-Caltech/University of Arizona, 7 (top, all), University of Colorado, 26; Science Source, 23, Walter Myers, 13; Shutterstock: AstroStar, interior space background, Rueangrit Srisuk, cover background; Sian Proctor/HI-SEAS, 28; Tunc Tezel, 7 (bottom); Wikipedia: Jean-Pol GRANDMONT, 6

Direct Quotations
Page 25 from NASA Solar System Exploration profile. solarsystem.nasa.gov/people/

Printed in Canada.
032015   008825FRF15

Table of Contents

Mysterious Mars.................................. 4
The Red One.................................... 6
Desert Planet................................... 8
The Secret of Seasons and Sols................. 10
Volcanoes, Craters, and Canyons................ 12
The First Photos............................... 16
Viking Searches for Life....................... 18
Rovers Travel Across Mars...................... 20
Curiosity's Unusual Landing.................... 22
Curiosity Looks for Answers.................... 24
Orbiters and Rovers Pave the Way............... 26
Get Ready for Life on Mars..................... 28

Glossary....................................... 30
Read More...................................... 31
Internet Sites................................. 31
Critical Thinking Using the Common Core........ 32
Index.. 32

Mysterious Mars

This rusty red planet has captured people's attention since ancient times. Mars is a terrestrial planet. It is made of rock and metal, like Earth, Mercury, and Venus. Today Mars is a cold, dry planet. But it's possible that it hasn't always been that way. For years scientists have searched for proof that water once flowed across Mars' surface. If it did, what caused Mars to lose its water? Was there ever life on Mars? These are just some of the secrets Mars holds.

The distance between Mars and Earth changes. They are closest every two years when they are about 34 million miles (55 million kilometers) apart. At their farthest distance, they are about 249 million miles (401 million km) apart.

Fast Facts

Distance from Sun: 142 million miles (229 million km)

Diameter: 4,212 miles (6,779 km)

Moons: 2

Rings: 0

Length of day: 24 hours and 37 minutes

Length of year: 687 Earth days

Earth
Mars

The Red One

Thousands of years ago, ancient astronomers discovered the planets in the sky. Mars stood out because of its reddish color. To the ancient Egyptians, Mars was "Har Decher," which means "the red one." They also called it the "backward traveler." It appeared to move in one direction in the sky for several months, then in the opposite direction.

To the Romans, the planet's red color reminded them of war. They named it Mars after the god of war.

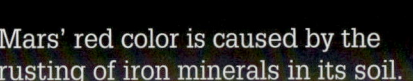
Mars

Mars' red color is caused by the rusting of iron minerals in its soil.

The ancient Greeks named Mars after their god of war, Ares. Mars' two moons were named after the horses that pulled Ares' chariot: Phobos and Deimos.

close-up images of tiny Phobos and Deimos

The Secret Behind the Backward Traveler

Mars' orbit doesn't actually change direction. The retrograde motion occurs when Earth passes Mars on its way around the Sun. As Mars falls behind, it appears to move temporarily backward in our sky.

Desert Planet

There is no life on Mars today because there is no liquid water. It is too cold, and Mars' atmosphere is too thin for liquid water to exist. Atmospheres surrounding Earth and Venus act like blankets and keep the planets warm. Mars' atmosphere is only 1/100th as thick as Earth's, and any water on Mars freezes.

There is water ice in some of Mars' *permanent* ice caps on its north and south poles. The *seasonal* ice caps on Mars' north and south poles are made up of carbon dioxide. It snows on Mars, but it's not made of water like snow on Earth. It snows carbon dioxide instead!

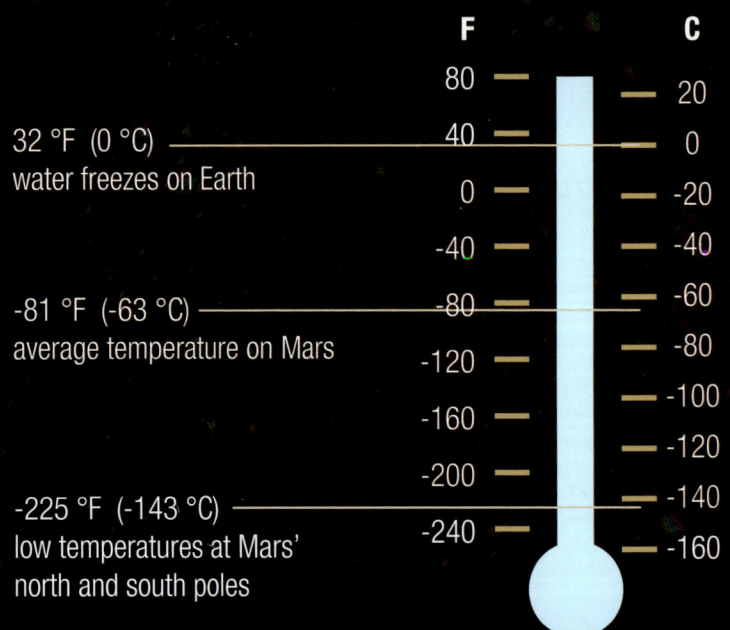

32 °F (0 °C) water freezes on Earth

-81 °F (-63 °C) average temperature on Mars

-225 °F (-143 °C) low temperatures at Mars' north and south poles

artist illustration of a dust storm on Mars

Global Dust Storms

Mars is dry and dusty like a desert. In the summer season, the Sun warms Mars' atmosphere. The heat causes the air to move, and winds lift dust off the ground. Dust storms are common. They can last for months and cover the entire planet.

The Secret of Seasons and Sols

Like Earth, Mars has four seasons. The seasonal polar ice caps on Mars, made of carbon dioxide, grow and shrink with Mars' seasons. In the winter Mars' north pole is tilted away from the Sun, and its polar ice caps expand. Meanwhile the south pole has summer, and its ice caps get smaller. But they don't melt like water ice would. Instead, the seasonal ice caps turn from solid carbon dioxide—"dry ice"—into a gas.

ice caps on Mars

Mars and Earth are the only planets with polar ice caps.

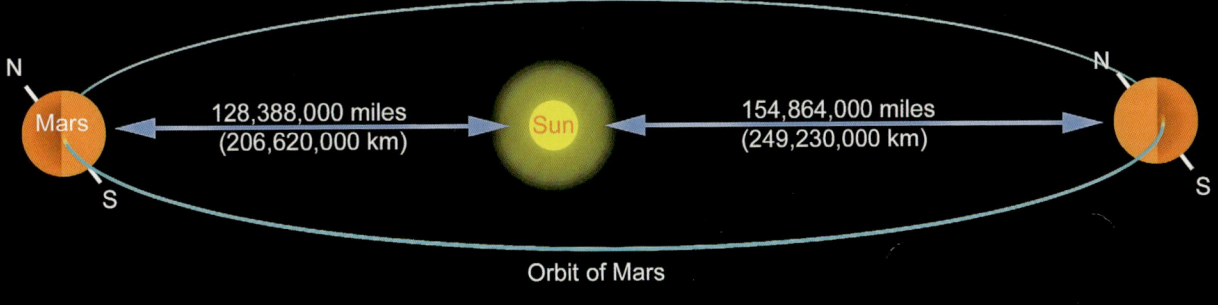

When Mars is close to the Sun, winter is mild in the northern hemisphere and summer is warm in the southern hemisphere.

When Mars is farthest from the Sun, summer is mild in the northern hemisphere, while winter is very cold in the southern hemisphere.

128,388,000 miles (206,620,000 km)

154,864,000 miles (249,230,000 km)

Orbit of Mars

Earth's almost circular orbit around the Sun means that each half of our planet receives about the same amount of solar heating each summer. Mars' orbit is less circular and more oval-shaped. This means that Mars' distance from the Sun changes. The weather of each season is affected by this change. Summer in Mars' southern hemisphere is warmer than summer in the northern hemisphere, because Mars is closer to the Sun at that time in its orbit.

One day on Mars is about 37 minutes longer than Earth's 24-hour day. A day on Mars is called a "sol."

One year on Mars is 687 Earth days, or 668.6 sols.

Volcanoes, Craters, and Canyons

Mars' surface is as varied as Earth's. It has hills, mountains, sandy plains, craters, volcanoes, and canyons. Over time, asteroids, volcanoes, dust storms, and perhaps even water may have caused Mars' surface to change. Scientists have been uncovering secrets on the surface of the red planet for decades.

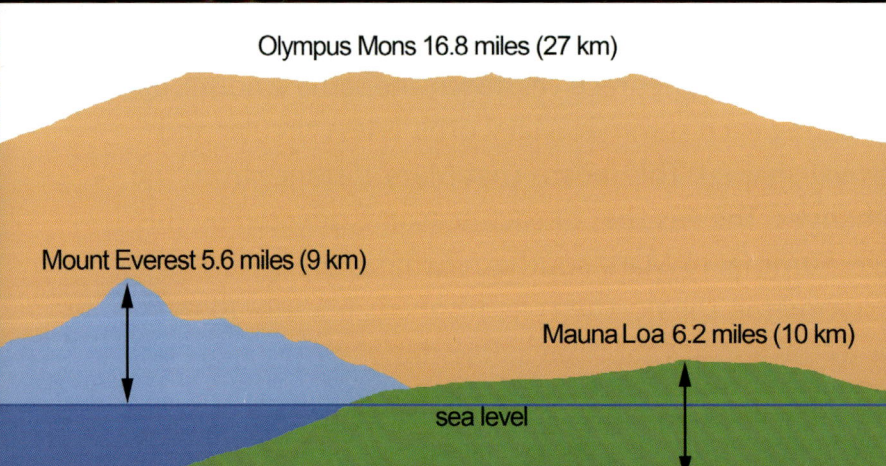

Olympus Mons 16.8 miles (27 km)

Mount Everest 5.6 miles (9 km)

Mauna Loa 6.2 miles (10 km)

sea level

Olympus Mons

Volcanoes

There are several giant volcanoes on Mars' surface. They are located in the Tharsis Montes region. Olympus Mons is the biggest volcano in the entire solar system. It is 100 times larger than the largest volcano on Earth, Hawaii's Mauna Loa. Olympus Mons juts 16 miles (26 km) up into the sky. Its base is 370 miles (600 km) across, which is about the same size as the state of Arizona.

Craters

Some areas of the planet are covered in craters that formed billions of years ago. Other craters were formed very recently. They come in various sizes and shapes. Gale Crater is 96 miles (154 km) across. Inside the crater is a mountain with rock layers that may date back billions of years. A smaller crater was found after an asteroid crashed into the planet in 2012. The crater would cover about half a football field.

Gale Crater

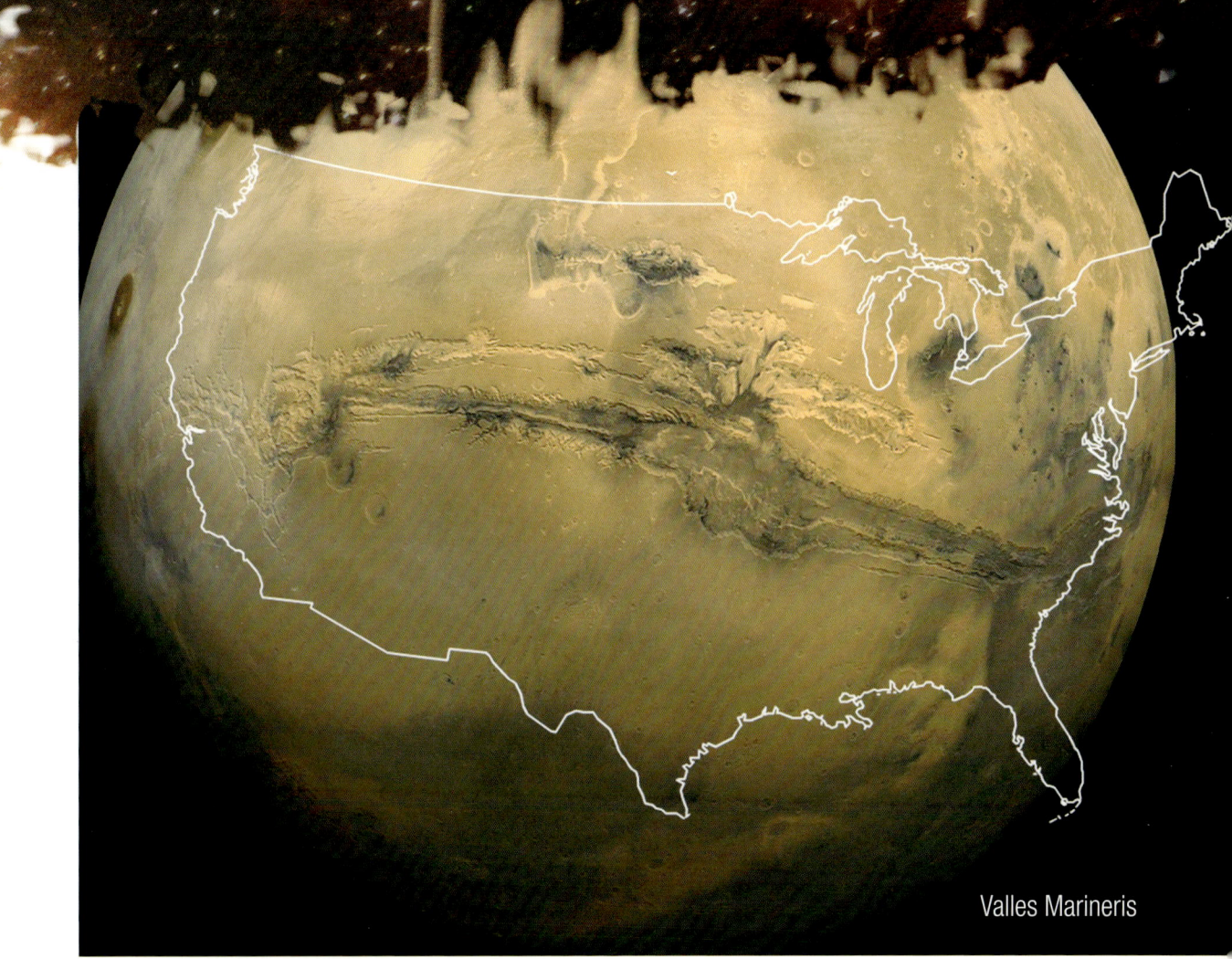

Valles Marineris

Valles Marineris

Mars is also home to the largest canyon in the solar system. Valles Marineris stretches 2,500 miles (4,000 km) across Mars. At its deepest, it extends 4 miles (6 km) into the ground. If it were on Earth, the canyon could stretch from Los Angeles to New York City. The Grand Canyon in Arizona is only 500 miles (800 km) long and 1 mile (1.6 km) deep.

Valles Marineris means Mariner Valley. Mariner 9 is the spacecraft that discovered it.

The First Photos

Humans have never been to Mars to uncover its mysteries in person. We continue to learn about the red planet through voyages of robotic spacecraft. The United States sent the first spacecraft to Mars in the 1960s. The first close-up photos of Mars were taken by Mariner 4 in July 1965 at a distance of 8,500 miles (13,680 km). Before Mariner 4 some people believed Mars could have water and even life. The photos showed that part of the planet looked more like the Moon than Earth.

Mariner 4 image of Mars' surface

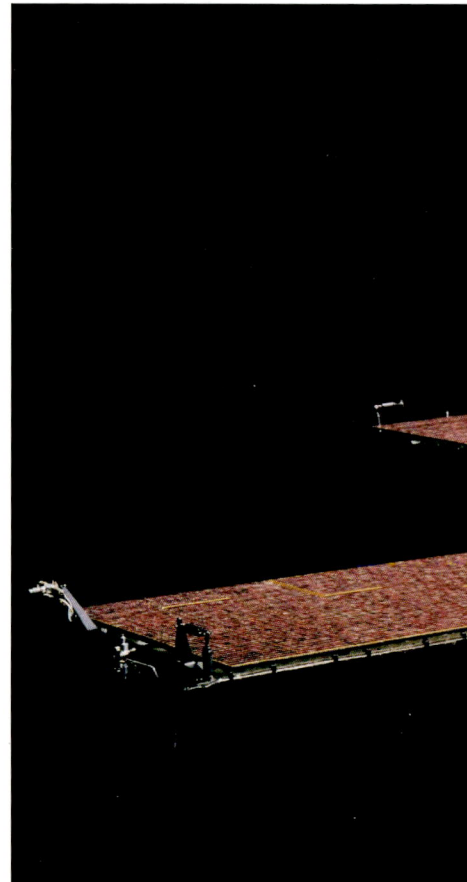

Mariner 9 orbited Mars in 1971. It was able to map 85 percent of the Martian surface. The new photos showed that half the planet is covered in volcanoes, canyons, and shallow valleys. The other half of Mars is covered in craters. None of the photos showed signs of water.

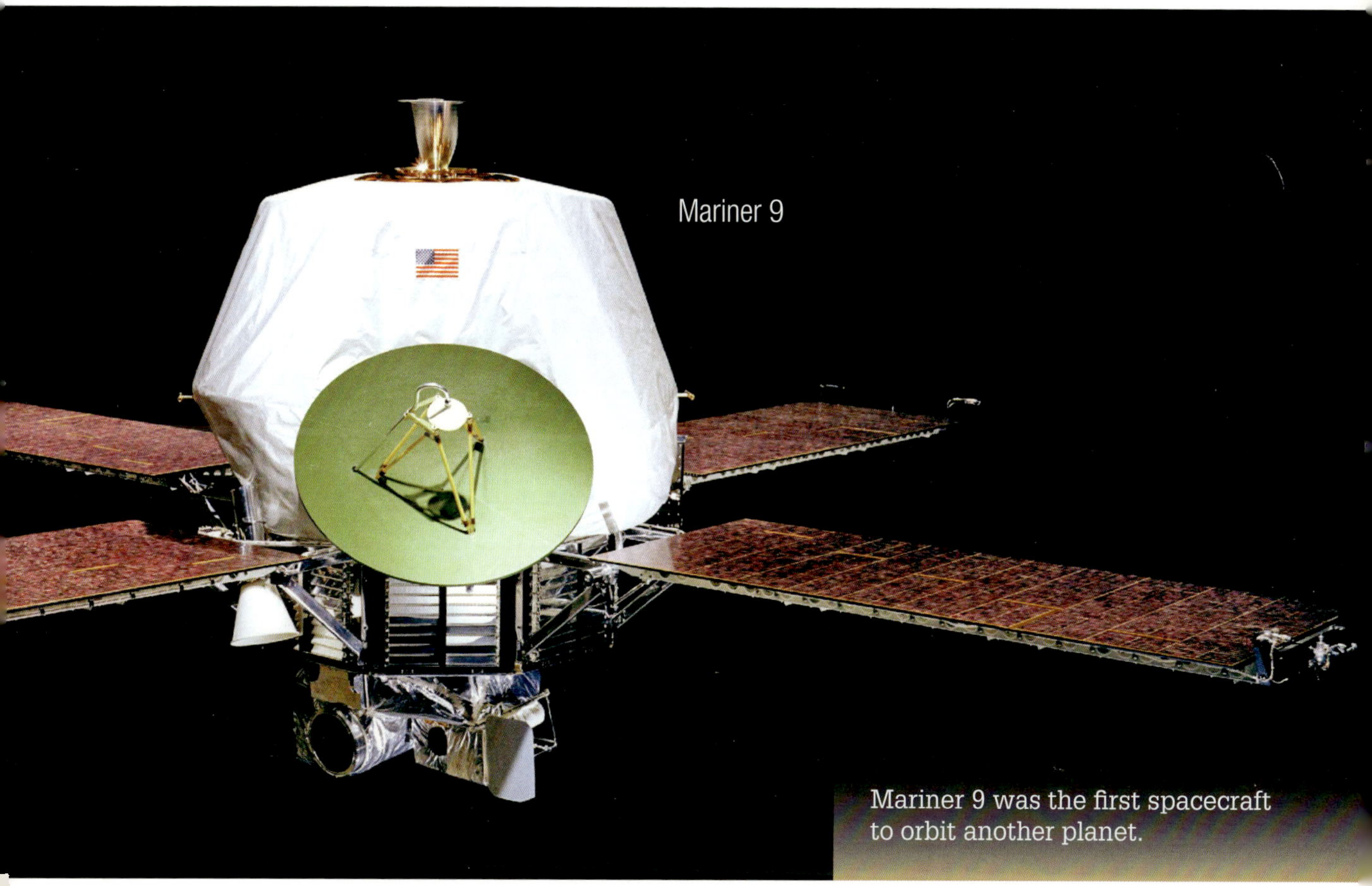

Mariner 9

Mariner 9 was the first spacecraft to orbit another planet.

17

Scientists still thought there was a possibility of water and small life forms just below the surface of Mars. Viking 1 and Viking 2 launched in 1975 to continue the search. They were the first spacecraft to land and send back information from Mars. The Viking spacecraft were identical and had two parts: an orbiter and a lander.

The orbiters were able to image the entire planet. They also took photographs of Phobos and Deimos, Mars' two moons. The landers took landscape photos from the surface and conducted experiments in search of life.

While no life was found, the Viking missions provided a huge leap forward in human understanding of Mars. But spacecraft did not successfully explore Mars again for 21 years.

view from Viking lander

The Smithsonian National Air and Space Museum opened in 1976 in Washington, D.C. Its official opening, called a "ribbon-cutting," began with a signal sent from the Viking spacecraft orbiting Mars. When the signal reached Earth, it caused a mechanical arm to cut the ribbon—"opening" the museum for the first time.

Rovers Travel Across Mars

The next time human technology landed on Mars, it was in the form of a rover. In space a rover is a computerized robot on wheels that explores the surface of a planet. The spacecraft Pathfinder used a large parachute to float to the surface of Mars in July 1997. It landed on a rocky area called Ares Vallis. Pathfinder released a microwave-sized rover named Sojourner. It was the first rover on Mars.

Twin exploration rovers Spirit and Opportunity landed on Mars in April 2004. Just months after landing, Opportunity found proof there was once salt water on the surface of Mars. Spirit found signs that water may have influenced volcanic rock and changed the surface. The rovers continued to explore Mars longer than expected. Spirit stopped sending signals back to Earth in 2010, but Opportunity was still exploring Mars in 2015.

Sojourner was named after American civil rights leader Sojourner Truth.

view from Spirit rover

Curiosity's Unusual Landing

The Mars Science Laboratory spacecraft launched in November 2011 and traveled for more than eight months. A rover was tucked inside. It was named Curiosity after its mission to uncover more secrets. Once it was close enough, a parachute helped to slow it down. Then rockets fired to slow the descent, and it lowered the rover down to the surface using three nylon ropes. Once Curiosity's wheels set down on Mars, the cables were cut. The module with the rockets zoomed off and crash-landed away from the rover.

Curiosity is 7 feet (2 meters) tall and weighs about 2,000 pounds (907 kilograms). That's two times longer and five times heavier than Spirit and Opportunity.

Curiosity rover lands on Mars

Curiosity has 17 cameras to take pictures of Mars' surface. It also has a laser and a drill to study the rocks on Mars.

Curiosity Looks for Answers

Curiosity

So far, Curiosity has revealed many of Mars' important secrets. Curiosity drove up a tall hill in Gale Crater to get a close look at exposed geological layers. Samples drilled from rocks found evidence that there was once liquid water and other elements necessary for life on Mars. Curiosity also measured radiation levels that are too high for human safety. Scientists will use that data when planning future missions.

Scientist Spotlight: Ashwin R. Vasavada

Ashwin Vasavada is the project scientist for the Curiosity rover. He leads a team of 500 people who plan how to use the rover's instruments and study the data it collects. Before accepting this leadership position, he was a research scientist for the Mars Science Laboratory. He's been involved with other NASA missions too, studying Jupiter, Saturn, and of course, Mars. After watching the Curiosity rover launch toward Mars he thought, "We really are just tiny human beings using all our intellectual and mechanical strength to sling ourselves virtually to other worlds."

Orbiters and Rovers Pave the Way

The MAVEN spacecraft entered Mars' orbit in September 2014. Its mission is to study how and why Mars' climate changed over time. MAVEN measures the solar wind around Mars to determine how it may be linked to Mars' loss of atmosphere. Evidence has already been found that there was once water and a thicker atmosphere on Mars. MAVEN is trying to determine why the atmosphere changed, and what happened to the water on Mars. It will also help to inform future missions to Mars.

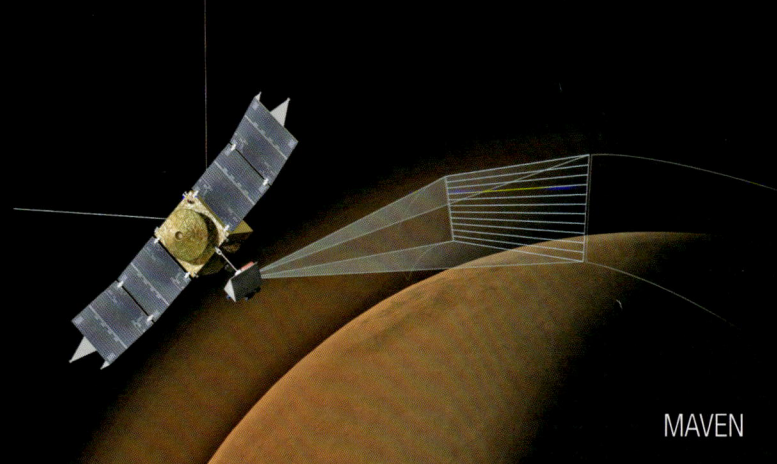

MAVEN

MAVEN stands for Mars Atmosphere and Volatile EvolutioN.

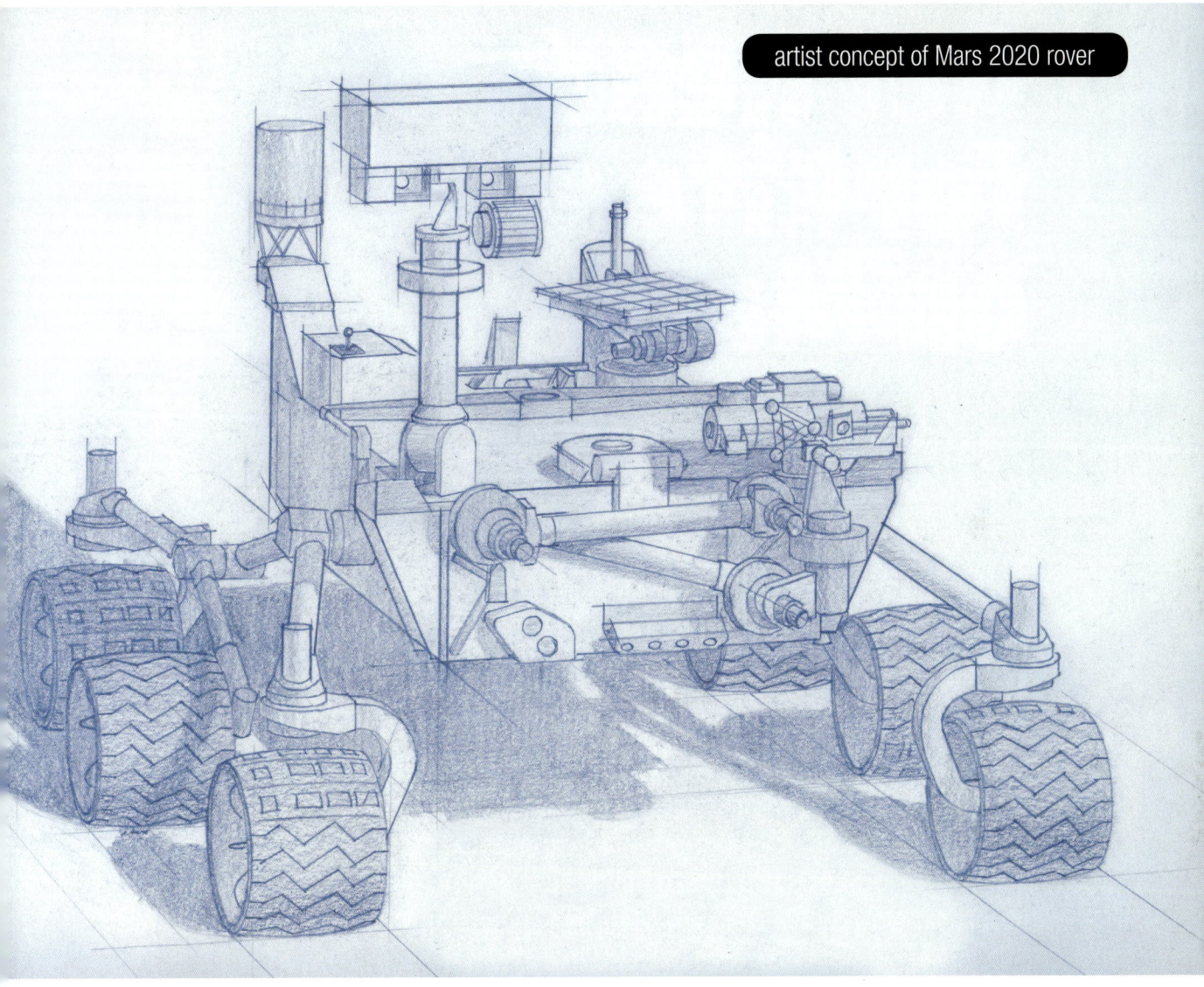

artist concept of Mars 2020 rover

The Mars 2020 Mission will use a rover with advanced tools to measure temperature, wind speed and direction, pressure, humidity, and dust particles. It will also experiment with making breathable oxygen from carbon dioxide in Mars' atmosphere. This technology is essential for human life support if people travel to Mars.

Get Ready for Life on Mars

Some people are already preparing for human travel to Mars. Six people finished a four-month stay in a dome on Hawaii's Mauna Loa volcano in July 2014. Another crew started an eight-month stay in October 2014. Their mission is to practice living in an environment similar to Mars. The two-story dome has a living and dining area, a lab, and exercise equipment on the first floor. The second floor has six small rooms and a bathroom. When the crew steps outside the dome, they have to wear spacesuits. However, they can't imitate the loss of gravity they would experience on Mars. Their practice also doesn't include the nine long months it would take to reach Mars in a spacecraft.

Mauna Loa dome

artist illustration of humans on Mars

It is possible that someday people could walk on Mars, even if it's a long way in the future. In the meantime we continue to learn more and more about the secrets of Mars.

Mars' gravity is much weaker than Earth's. If you weighed 100 pounds (45 kg) on Earth, you'd weigh only 37.7 pounds (17 kg) on Mars!

Glossary

asteroid (AS-tuh-royd)—a small rocky body that orbits the Sun

astronomy (uh-STRAH-nuh-mee)—the study of stars, planets, and space

atmosphere (AT-muhss-fihr)—the mixture of gases that surrounds a planet or moon

carbon dioxide (KAR-buhn dye-OK-side)—a gas that is a mixture of carbon and oxygen, with no color or odor

crater (KRAY-tuhr)—a large hole in the ground caused by something such as a bomb or meteorite

gravity (GRAV-uh-tee)—the force that pulls things down or to the center of a planet and keeps them from floating away into space

hemisphere (HEM-uhss-fihr)—one half of a sphere, especially of a planet

module (MOJ-ool)—a separate, independent section that can be linked to other parts to make something larger, as in a space module

orbit (OR-bit)—the invisible path followed by an object circling a planet, the Sun, etc.

polar ice cap (POH-lur)—a mound of ice that covers an area of land and gets bigger as snow falls, melts, and freezes, located in the region around the north or south pole

radiation (RAY-dee-AY-shuhn)—energy that comes from a source in the form of waves or rays that you cannot see; can be dangerous energy

retrograde (REH-truh-greyd)—having a backward motion or direction

robot (ROH-bot)—a machine that is programmed to do jobs that are usually performed by a person

solar wind (SOH-lur)—a stream of particles released from the Sun

terrestrial (tuh-RESS-tree-uhl)—describes a planet with land, like Earth and Mars

Read More

Carson, Mary Kay. *Far-Out Guide to Mars.* Berkeley Heights, New Jersey: Enslow Publishers, Inc., 2011.

Oxlade, Chris. *Mars.* Chicago: Capstone Global Library, Ltd., 2013.

Squire, Ann. *Planet Mars.* New York: Scholastic, 2014.

Internet Sites

FactHound offers a safe, fun way to find Internet sites related to this book. All of the sites on FactHound have been researched by our staff.

Here's all you do:

Visit www.facthound.com

Type in this code: 9781491458655

FactHound will fetch the best sites for you!

Check out projects, games and lots more at
www.capstonekids.com

Critical Thinking Using the Common Core

1. Read the text on page 18. How do orbiters and landers collect different information? (Key Ideas and Details)

2. Read the text and look at the images on pages 28 and 29. How are people preparing for life on Mars? What benefits could come from sending humans to Mars instead of only rovers? (Integration of Knowledge and Ideas)

Index

Ares Vallis, 20
atmosphere, 8, 26–27

backward traveler, 6–7

craters, 12, 14, 16–17
Curiosity rover, 22–25

desert, 4, 9
dust storms, 9

Gale Crater, 14, 25

humans on Mars, 27–29

ice caps, 8, 10–11
inner planets, 4, 8

life on Mars, 4, 16, 18, 25

Mariner 4, 16
Mariner 9, 15, 17
Mars 2020 Mission, 27
Mars Science Laboratory, 22, 25
Mauna Loa volcano, 12–13, 28
MAVEN, 26
moons, 5–7, 18
mythology, 6–7

National Air and Space Museum, 19

Opportunity rover, 20
orbiters, 18, 26

Pathfinder, 20

red color, 4, 6–7
rovers, 20–21, 26–27

seasons, 10–11
Sojourner, 20
solar wind, 26
sols, 11
spacecraft, 16–28
Spirit rover, 20–21

temperatures, 4, 8
terrestrial, 4
topography, 12–16, 20

Valles Marineris, 15
Vasavada, Ashwin, 25
Viking 1 & 2, 18–19

water, 4, 8, 12, 16, 20, 25, 26